World Issues

ABORTION

Beth Bacon

Chrysalis Children's Books

WORLD ISSUES

ABORTION	EQUAL OPPORTUNITIES	HUMAN RIGHTS
ANIMAL RIGHTS	EUTHANASIA	POVERTY
ARMS TRADE	FOOD TECHNOLOGY	RACISM
CAPITAL PUNISHMENT	GENETIC ENGINEERING	REFUGEES
CONSUMERISM	GENOCIDE	TERRORISM
DRUGS		

First published in the UK in 2004 by
Chrysalis Children's Books
An imprint of Chrysalis Books Group PLC
The Chrysalis Building, Bramley Road, London W10 6SP

Produced by Tall Tree Ltd

Editorial Manager: Joyce Bentley
Editors: Clare Lewis and Joe Fullman
Project Editor: Jon Richards
Designer: Ben Ruocco
Picture Researcher: Lorna Ainger
Consultant: Dr Sue Mann

ISBN: 1 84458 082 2

British Library Cataloguing in Publication Data for this book is available from the British Library.
Printed in China

10 9 8 7 6 5 4 3 2 1

Picture Acknowledgments

The Publishers would like to thank the following for their permission to reproduce the photographs:
AKG London: 24
Alamy: Michel Friang 26, Robert Harding Picture Library 45, Jacques Jangoux 9c, Ian Thraves 29
Art Archive: Bibliothèque des Arts Décoratifs Paris/Dagli Orti 14
Corbis: 12, Bettmann 16, 17, 33, 47, Najlah Feanny/SABA 51, Owen Franken 38, Tom & Dee Ann McCarthy 11, Will & Deni McIntyre 8-9, Roy McMahon 28, Russell Underwood 9t
Eye Ubiquitous: Hutchinson Library 44
Getty Images: Mario Tama 41, 50
The Miami Herald: 35
PA Photos: Abaca Press 48, Barry Batchelor 27, EPA 23
Popperfoto: Reuters 32, 34, 42
Rex Features Ltd. 15, Sipa Press 22, 39
Science Photo Library: 7, 13, 46, Neil Bromhall 20, Colin Cuthbert front cover, 36, GE Medical Systems 43, Gary Parker 31, Lea Paterson 10, James Stevenson 19, Jim Varney 37, Andy Walker/Midland Fertility Services 18
Still Pictures: Ron Giling 9b, Knut Mueller 21, Shehzad Noorani 25, Sean Sprague 5, 30
Topham: ImageWorks 49, UN 40

CONTENTS

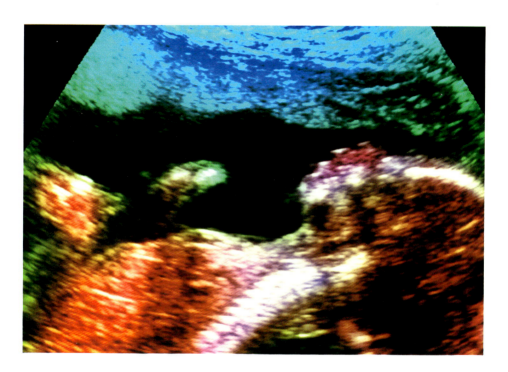

Karla's Story

Karla (her name has been changed) was a 14 year-old girl who lived in the Republic of Ireland. In 1992, she was raped by the father of one of her school friends and became pregnant. The Irish constitution forbids abortion, but every year thousands of Irish women travel to the UK, where abortions became legal in 1967.

KARLA PLEADED WITH her parents to take her to London for an abortion and they agreed. Because of the trial of her school friend's father, the family told the Irish police what they were going to do. This resulted in a legal uproar in Ireland and the case, taken up by the media, was broadcast nationally and internationally.

Many people felt that the girl should be allowed to have an abortion in spite of the laws prohibiting it. Because she had been raped, an exception should be made. Lawyers, however, continued to argue the case in court. Eventually, the Irish High Court ruled that Karla had no legal right to end her pregnancy. Instead, they decided that the rights of her unborn baby had to be protected.

The Irish police telephoned the girl's family in London and demanded that they return to Ireland without having the abortion. By now, Karla was extremely distressed and contemplating suicide. There was a wave of national and international public protest and sympathy on her behalf. Huge crowds marched through the streets, showing their support for Karla and calling for a change in the Irish abortion laws.

Finally, after several difficult weeks, the court ruled that Karla could have the abortion in London, because her suicide threats proved that her life was in danger. However, the court also made it clear that Karla's case did not change Ireland's laws. Abortion was still illegal there, except to save a woman's life, and it remains so today.

Abortion around the world

The rules surrounding abortion differ in various countries around the world.

THE NETHERLANDS
A young woman from the Netherlands. In this country, abortion rates are very low because women can get cheap, safe contraception and receive good sex education in school.

BRAZIL
In Brazil, the world's most populous Roman Catholic country, abortion is illegal except in cases of rape or grave risk to the mother. Nevertheless, women's groups estimate that Brazilian women undergo an estimated one million abortions every year, and prosecution is rare.

ZAMBIA
A woman from Zambia, which was the first country in Africa south of the Sahara to make abortions legal. But the country is so poor that there are not enough doctors to perform them.

What is Abortion?

Abortion is a medical term that means ending a pregnancy. An abortion can happen naturally. This is known as a miscarriage or spontaneous abortion. Abortion can also be induced (caused unnaturally) by controlled medical treatment, or by illegal 'back-street' and home-made procedures.

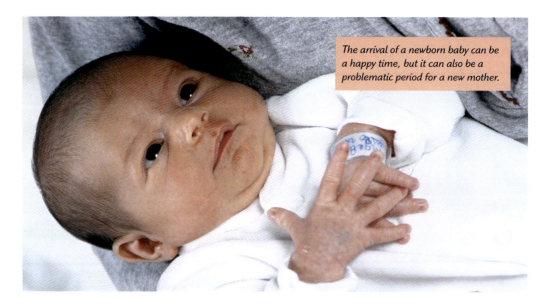

The arrival of a newborn baby can be a happy time, but it can also be a problematic period for a new mother.

EVERY DAY, WOMEN throughout the world actively seek an abortion as a way of ending a pregnancy. What leads them to decide that abortion is the better option? Is this decision emotionally painful for a woman? The reasons for abortion are diverse, as we will discover later in the book.

How many abortions happen every year?

There are an estimated 45 million abortions performed worldwide every year. This compares to an estimated 128.6 million births per year. Some 20 million of these abortions are performed illegally. Why do so many

women throughout the world resort to a criminal act to terminate a pregnancy? And what kind of health risks are involved? We will look at the cases of abortion in countries that prohibit the practice and at other cases in parts of the world that tolerate abortion. Some statistics are surprising: why, for example, is the abortion rate generally lower in countries where it is practised legally?

Even in countries where abortion is legal, people's opinions on the practice are divided. Some, for example pro-life groups (see page 40), believe that life begins at the very start of a pregnancy, and that, therefore, abortion is a form of murder. The opposing argument is that a pregnant woman's right to choose whether or not to have an abortion should be respected (see page 36). Who should have the final decision: society, doctors or the woman herself? Or should the unborn foetus' right to life be most important? These issues will be discussed in the following chapters.

We will also look at how advances in medical science and embryology affect abortion practice and at the course of abortion legislation throughout history to the present day. There are also moral and ethical questions surrounding abortion in the light of medical and religious opinion, as well as social and economic factors in different cultures worldwide which need to be looked at.

Abortion worldwide

One recent report estimates that 25 million women have legal abortions and about 20 million have illegal abortions each year. The estimated current global monthly average is 1 227 000 abortions. Around 78 per cent of all abortions are obtained in developing countries and 22 per cent occur in developed countries. Worldwide, the lifetime average is about one abortion per woman.

Source: *Sharing Responsibility: Women, Society and Abortion Worldwide* Alan Guttmacher Institute

Pregnant women have to deal with a great many issues in deciding whether to progress with or teminate a pregnancy.

Has Abortion Always Existed?

The practice of abortion has existed since ancient times. The Assyrians and Babylonians, who lived 4000 years ago in the Middle East, punished women who had abortions. In Ancient Israel, anyone who assisted a woman in aborting her foetus was a criminal. In Ancient Egypt, however, abortion was not against the law.

THERE ARE MEDICAL texts dating from 1300 BC which record concoctions of herbs, spices and animal dung that were used by women as contraceptives and to induce an abortion. Ancient Greek and Roman texts, over 2000 years old, also show evidence of powerful drugs and violent exercises being used by women as a means of aborting a foetus.

Have people always wondered when human life begins?

The Ancient Greek philosopher Aristotle (384–322 BC) taught that a foetus originally has a vegetable soul. This evolves into an animal soul during the early stages of pregnancy before finally becoming animated, or brought to life, with a human soul. This belief

Hippocrates is associated with the Hippocratic oath, which all medical students swear on graduating.

Hippocrates

The Ancient Greek doctor Hippocrates (c. 460–377 BC) is often called the Father of Medicine. He taught that it was wrong to give medicine to induce an abortion.

Using his early microscope, Antonie von Leeuwenhoek was the first person to study and describe many human body cells accurately, including sperm and blood.

DEBATE – Should religion govern abortion issues?

• Yes. Abortion is a moral issue concerning life and death. It therefore forms an important part of any religious teaching in any culture.

• No. The choice to have an abortion is a personal decision for the woman and should not be decided by the teachings of an organised religion.

was called delayed ensoulment and was widely accepted at the time. It was believed to occur at 40 days after conception for male foetuses and 90 days after conception for female foetuses. So abortion was not condemned if it was performed early in gestation. But if an abortion was done later in pregnancy, then people believed a human soul had been destroyed.

What were the attitudes upheld by other religions in the past?

Muslim beliefs on the sanctity of life have varied throughout history. Traditionally, Islam has believed that a foetus becomes a person before birth, but Muslims have not always agreed as to when this occurs. Some medieval authorities record it as happening at 120 days of gestation, after which abortion was considered an act of murder.

The Ancient Hebrew belief was that the foetus did not have the same moral status as a person and human life was only achieved at birth. Later, however, embryonic and foetal life were more valued, and abortion was permitted only when the mother's physical health was at risk, or in cases of serious foetal abnormality.

Did science play a role in changing religious attitudes in Europe?

In 1677, Antonie von Leeuwenhoek, a pioneer Dutch microscope-maker, was the first person to observe moving sperm under a microscope. His discoveries led to a confused debate among scientists and theologians. If sperm were living organisms outside the womb, did life begin, therefore, at the moment of conception inside the womb? Scientific confusion was also caused when two 17th-century physicians, Thomas Fienus of Louvain, Belgium, and Paolo Zacchia of Rome, claimed that a rational soul existed from the moment of conception. They thought they had seen fully formed human shapes in early embryos while peering through primitive microscopes.

Eugenics

Eugenics is the belief that the human race can be improved through selective breeding and birth control techniques. Supporters of eugenics surfaced during the 19th century with the likes of Francis Galton, a cousin of Charles Darwin, who pioneered the Eugenics Movement in 1883. This movement sought to preserve a fit and healthy population not only by maintaining strict anti-abortion laws, but also by enforcing birth control and the sterilisation of those deemed inferior and therefore unfit to reproduce.

What changes occurred in the 19th century?

The 19th century saw significant changes in attitudes towards abortion, resulting in new legislation and greater severity of punishments. In 1869, the Catholic Church under Pope Pius IX declared a total ban on abortion, proclaiming that life with a soul started at the moment of conception. Abortion was punished by excommunication, the church's most severe penalty. In England and the United States, strict anti-abortion laws were passed, making abortion punishable by death in some cases.

The factories of the Industrial Revolution needed a large workforce to work in them.

In the mid-19th century there was an effort to tighten abortion regulation, led, in part, by the medical community. By the late 1860s, uniform abortion prohibition had been established in England and throughout most of the United States. These laws would remain in place in all 50 states until the 1960s. In the state of New Jersey, USA, for example, the penalty for anybody assisting in an abortion ranged from fines of up to US$5000 to a 15-year prison sentence.

How were European colonies influenced?

This new intolerance extended to the European colonies in Asia, Africa, South America and the Caribbean. Spain's strict anti-abortion laws were reflected in many statutes decreed in their South American colonies, for example. Towards the end of the 19th century, China and Japan, which were under the

In the middle of the 20th century, the rise of the Women's Rights Movement saw an increase in protests demanding the relaxation of abortion laws.

influence of Western powers at the time, also criminalised abortion.

There was another motive behind the anti-abortion laws of the 19th century. The Western world was in the grip of the Industrial Revolution and factories needed more and more workers to increase production. It was imperative, therefore, that women produce as many children as possible to increase the workforce. Unchecked, abortion would lead to a shortage of workers and subsequent economic disaster. European governments also needed a steady supply of people to work in their colonial lands.

In response to the rise of pro-choice protests, an anti-abortion movement formed, protesting for the rights of the unborn child.

What happened in the 20th Century?

Women, rich and poor, continued to seek abortions illegally, however. Thousands died or were seriously injured through unsanitary and dangerous abortion methods. During the 1950s and 1960s, the rise of the Women's Rights Movement pushed the abortion debate to the forefront. Greater sexual freedom in the 1960s led to an increase in illegal abortions. Abortionists often turned women away if they could not pay US$1000 or more in cash. Pro-choice groups lobbied governments to liberalise the laws. In the United States, inspired by the Civil Rights and Antiwar movements, women began to fight more

actively for their rights. They marched and rallied for 'abortion on demand'. Similar demonstrations took place in the UK. The British government responded with the Abortion Act of 1967, which came into effect in 1968. This allowed a pregnancy to be terminated under certain conditions and with the consent of two doctors.

Also in 1967, two American states, Colorado and California, introduced laws to legalise abortion for a very wide range of medical reasons. In 1970, the state of New York passed the first law allowing abortion on demand up to the 24th week of pregnancy. However,

Justice Harry Blackmun was responsible for delivering the majority verdict in the Roe v Wade case which legalised abortion in the US.

illegal abortion remained common since the laws were still restrictive for many women. Then came the 1973 Roe v Wade Supreme Court ruling on abortion which held that women have a constitutional right to decide whether or not to terminate a pregnancy. This enabled the legalisation of abortion across the United States. An important later piece of legislation in the UK was the Human Fertilisation and Embryology Act of 1990. This introduced a time limit of 24 weeks for an abortion under certain circumstances and no limit for others. Before this change, a 28-week limit had applied to all grounds for abortion.

How did anti-abortion supporters react to these changes?

The Roe v Wade ruling energised the anti-abortion lobby. They began to demonstrate, using clinic blockades, legislative strategies and legal challenges.

The first victory for anti-abortion campaigners came in July 1976, when the US Congress passed the Hyde Amendment. This banned Medicaid (government) funding for an abortion unless a woman's life was in danger. After this was passed, many US states stopped funding abortions unless they were considered medically necessary.

When Does Life Begin?

The question of when life begins forms one of the central issues behind the abortion debate. Does life begin at conception, the very start of a pregnancy, or does it only start when the baby is born? In this chapter, we will examine the different stages of pregnancy and look at different views about when life begins.

CONCEPTION IS A process involving three separate stages: fertilisation (the joining together of male and female reproductive cells); division; and implantation. A woman needs to conceive in order to get pregnant. From puberty, humans produce cells for reproduction. The male cells are sperm, stored in a man's testes. The female cells are eggs, stored in a woman's ovaries. Both the male and female sex cells contain the genetic information needed to make up the cells in the human body. For fertilisation to occur the eggs and sperm must join together. When a man and woman have sexual intercourse without using safe contraception, one sperm can fuse with a single egg. If fertilisation does not occur, then the unfertilised egg is released from the woman's body, along with the built-up lining of the womb, in what is referred to as a period or menstruation. This occurs once every 28 days or so.

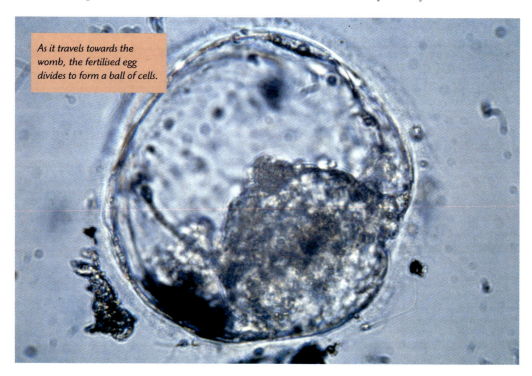

As it travels towards the womb, the fertilised egg divides to form a ball of cells.

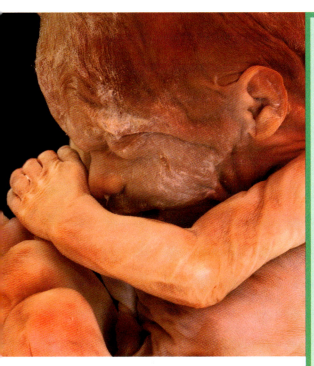

About 12–15 weeks after fertilisation, the foetus is about 60 mm in length.

From egg to foetus

There are many different names for cells formed during conception and pregnancy:
- An egg cell that has been fertilised by a sperm cell is called a zygote.
- A cluster of cells, formed when a zygote divides, is called a morula. This occurs roughly three days after fertilisation.
- A morula forms into a hollow sphere called a blastocyst. This occurs four to five days after fertilisation.
- About a day later, the blastocyst implants into the lining of the uterus.
- Approximately eight weeks after implantation, the embryo starts to look recognisably human. For the rest of the pregnancy, it is called a foetus.
- Once the foetus is born, it is called a baby.

What happens after fertilisation?

As soon as an egg is fertilised, it starts to grow. It splits into two cells, which continue dividing to form a hollow cluster. After about five days, this grows tiny 'fingers' around its outer edge which burrow into the lining of a woman's uterus, or womb. This is called implantation. If the cluster of cells fails to implant in the uterus, it dies. But if implantation succeeds, the cluster feeds from the uterus' rich blood supply, and it grows very quickly. It develops into a minute creature, called an embryo, which is protected by a surrounding fluid-filled bag. The embryo is linked to the wall of the uterus by an umbilical cord and an organ called the placenta.

When can a woman have an abortion?

If a woman misses her period after sexual intercourse there is a strong possibility that she has conceived and is pregnant.

Usually, she will do a home pregnancy test, followed up by a pregnancy test at a clinic. A pregnancy is measured from the time of the woman's last period and, if carried to completion, will last for approximately 40 weeks. The majority of abortions are carried out in the first 12 weeks of a pregnancy, with very few occurring after 20 weeks. In the UK, for example, almost 90 per cent of abortions are in the first 12 weeks of pregnancy, and just 1.5 per cent are after 20 weeks. In the USA, 91 per cent of all abortions occur within the first 12 weeks of pregnancy, 98 per cent within 15 weeks and 99.9 per cent within 27 weeks.

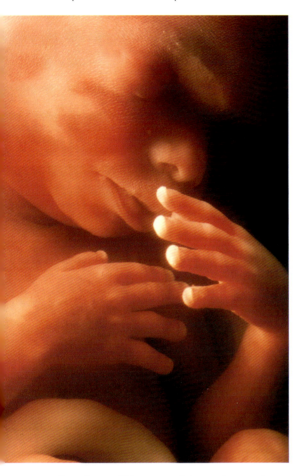

At 20 weeks after conception, the foetus measures about 112 mm from the top of the head to the rump.

Are there different opinions about when life begins?

Societies and organisations around the world hold different beliefs on the question of when life begins. Opinions range from the belief that life begins at the moment of fertilisation, to others that believe that life cannot be said to start until the child has been born. In between these two extremes are several stages where certain groups believe a human being starts their existence. These include 'quickening', the time when the baby first moves in the womb, or at viability, when the foetus can survive outside the mother's womb.

What do Christians believe?

The Roman Catholic Church teaches that human life begins when the woman's egg is fertilised by a man's sperm. A unique life begins at that moment, independent of the life of the mother and father. This is a human being with potential not just a potential human being. The Christian view is that this life deserves the same the value, rights and protection that are granted an infant, child or adult. Some Christians maintain the Bible's teachings of life before birth. For them, God is both the creator and a sacred presence in the unborn child.

Other Christian denominations, such as the Churches of England and Scotland, also place paramount importance on the sanctity of all human life, including that of the unborn child. However, they also permit abortion in exceptional cases, for example, when the pregnancy threatens the life of the mother.

What does Buddhism teach its followers?

The early scriptures of Buddhism teach that human life starts with conception. If this is so, then an abortion is seen as morally wrong because it breaks one of the basic laws of Buddhism, which is to abstain from harming or killing living beings. Some branches of Buddhism, however, tolerate abortion under certain circumstances.

When do other religions say that life begins?

In Hindu tradition and philosophy abortion is forbidden, except when the life of the mother is threatened. The Hindu faith believes that the soul enters the womb at the time of conception. Abortion is called *garbha batta* or 'womb killing' or *brhoona hathya*, meaning 'killing the undeveloped soul'.

Judaism teaches that life begins at birth, although abortion is discouraged except where the mother's life is at risk. The foetus has great value because it is potentially a human life, but it will only gain full human status at birth.

In Islamic teaching, a soul enters the foetus not at the moment of conception, but at 120 days. However, abortion is still only permitted in extreme circumstances, and early abortion is definitely preferred.

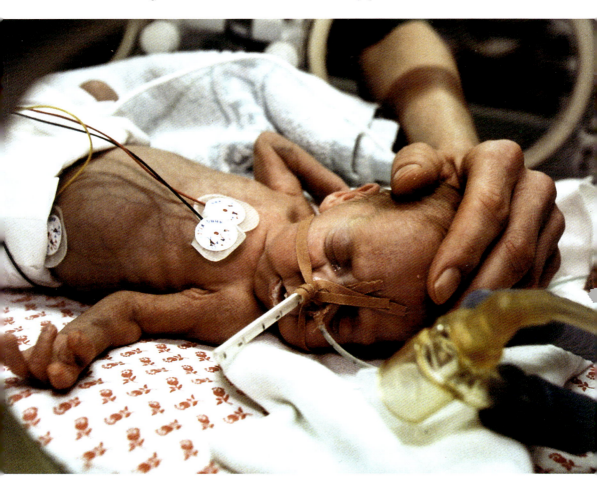

A premature baby in intensive care. Improvements in medical technology have shifted the time of viability, when the infant can survive outside the womb.

How Does Abortion Happen?

There are several procedures available for deliberately ending a pregnancy. Women can have a medical abortion or a surgical one. Although these are normally straightforward methods, some people are concerned about the possible physical, psychological and emotional effects.

AN ABORTION CAN happen naturally, when it is called a miscarriage, or it can be induced deliberately. There are several different abortion procedures according to the stage of the pregnancy.

In early medical abortion, up to nine weeks, drugs are used. The regime of drugs differs from one country to another. In the USA, the two drugs used are methotrexate and misoprostol. Methotrexate is given by injection and stops the embryo's cells from dividing, thereby preventing further development. Misoprostol is then inserted into the vagina, often by the woman at home, five to seven days after the first medication. This drug causes the womb to contract. The woman experiences cramping and bleeding and the embryo is usually expelled within a week.

What are the other methods?

From about weeks seven to 13 of a pregnancy, a method called 'vacuum aspiration' is commonly used. A woman can sometimes choose to have this under local or general anaesthetic. Many hospitals and clinics prefer to use a general anaesthetic. During a vacuum aspiration abortion, a thin tube is eased into the uterus through the cervix (the passage that links the vagina to the womb). By using a gentle pump, the contents of the uterus pass out of the womb and into the tube.

For a longer gestation, usually weeks 15 to 19, a surgical procedure known as 'dilation and evacuation' is used. At

Another abortion drug is the RU-486 pill, or mifepristone. It also goes under the name Mifeprex.

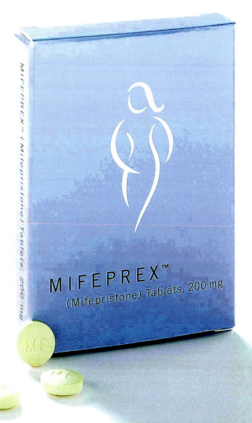

女援助中心

Legal abortions are carried out in specialised units, such as this one, by trained professionals.

this stage the foetus is too large to remove by suction without causing harm to the mother. The woman is given a light, general anaesthetic. The doctor then gently stretches the passage through the cervix. When it is wide enough, forceps are used to remove most of the contents of the womb. A vacuum pump is then used to clear out any remaining tissue.

Between weeks 20 and 24, a surgical two-stage abortion or a medical induction is used. During a medical induction, the fetal heart is usually stopped and then the doctor uses drugs to induce premature labour. A surgical two-stage abortion involves two operations to remove the contents of the womb.

Emergency contraceptives

The emergency pill is offered to women as an emergency contraceptive. It is, in fact, a series of pills and is one of the few forms of contraception that are taken after intercourse, when it acts to either delay the release of an egg from the ovaries or to prevent the implantation of the fertilised egg. The availability of the pill has caused deep controversy and is opposed by pro-life organisations which see it as a quick and casual method of abortion because its effect can occur after fertilisation.

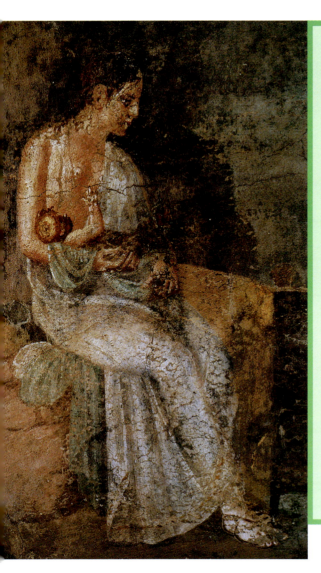

Abortion fatalities

The number of women who die worldwide from unsafe abortions annually is estimated to be between 70 000 and 200 000. This means that up to 20 per cent of maternal deaths are due to unsafe abortions. In Zimbabwe, where abortion is illegal, women are 262 times more likely to die from the procedure than women in the UK. In Asia, 57 per cent of all female deaths are thought to be caused by illegal abortions. In Bangladesh, 80 per cent of women do not have access to safe abortion procedures.

Sources: *Our Bodies, Ourselves for the New Century* Boston Women's Health Book Collective, WHO data

In ancient times, it was common for women in their early twenties to die in childbirth.

Is abortion dangerous?

Legal abortions are usually very safe when performed by trained medical staff in hygienic surroundings. Statistics in the UK show that a woman is over seven times as likely to die as a result of a full-term pregnancy than from the termination of a pregnancy. There is a death rate of one in every 100 000–200 000 procedures. Serious physical problems during an abortion are rare and occur in one or two out of every 1000 abortions. Statistics in the USA show that when carried out by qualified doctors, legal abortions are more than ten times safer than giving birth.

More common are minor complications that occur during the procedure. In the UK, around one per cent of abortions are repeated because fragments of the pregnancy remain in the uterus. About ten per cent of women suffer pain or bleeding in the first month after an abortion. Up to two per cent of women who have an abortion get an infection after the procedure, which has to be treated with antibiotics.

Some pro-life groups, such as Feminists for Life, claim that legal abortion can lead to a number of serious physical complications such as cervical injury, an increased risk of breast cancer, a decrease in a woman's fertility and a 200 per cent increased risk of miscarriage after two abortions or more. These claims, however, cannot be proven scientifically or medically and studies of the long-term physical effects of abortion show that it does not affect later pregnancies or reduce fertility.

What about the rates for illegal abortions?

In countries where abortion is illegal, however, the death rates are much higher, and at least 70 000 women die from unsanitary abortions every year.

In some countries, such as Argentina, Brazil, Colombia, Dominican Republic, Indonesia, Nigeria, Philippines, Spain and South Africa, misoprostol (see page 22) is readily available on the black market. In most of these countries, women cannot obtain legal abortions. They buy the medication in order to terminate their pregnancies secretly, without medical help. The drug can often be purchased very cheaply, over the counter, requiring no prescription. Up to 75 per cent of clandestine abortions in Brazil involve the medication. When misoprostol is taken in isolation, it only causes an abortion about 40 per cent of the time. If the pregnancy continues, the baby will almost certainly be born with serious birth defects.

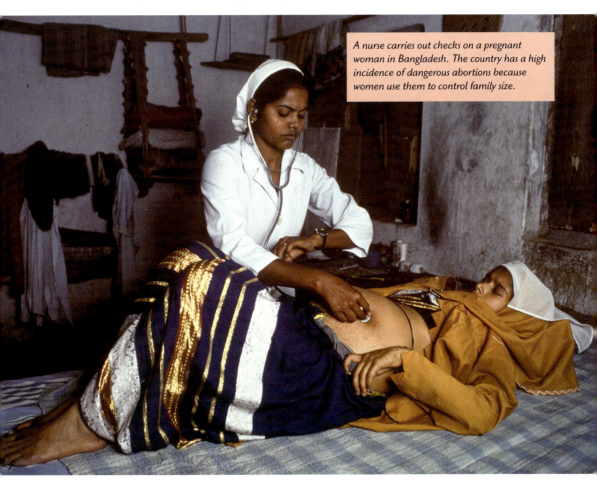

A nurse carries out checks on a pregnant woman in Bangladesh. The country has a high incidence of dangerous abortions because women use them to control family size.

Does abortion cause psychological and emotional problems?

The psychological and emotional effects of having an abortion can vary greatly from woman to woman. A decision to end a pregnancy is not always an easy one to make and the woman may feel a certain degree of sadness even though she sees the abortion as necessary. The feelings experienced after an abortion can range from sheer relief and liberation to a deep, inexpressible grief and regret. Studies in the UK have shown that about three per cent of women harbour long-term feelings of loss and guilt, some feeling that the abortion was a mistake.

Consideration should be given to the women who wanted to continue their pregnancy but, due to a malformation or congenital defect in the foetus, had to undergo a termination. A late-term abortion in these circumstances can add significantly to a woman's distress.

Some women may feel they need to talk to a post-abortion counsellor. This can help them to acknowledge fully any feelings of loss they have and, although they may feel very emotional after the abortion, the counselling can be extremely therapeutic. Feelings of anger can also emerge, directed at the woman herself or perhaps at her partner, and relationships may break up after an abortion.

Offering for the unborn

In Japan, some women who have had abortions make offerings at Buddha statues that represent 'Jizo' the 'Buddha of aborted babies'. This way, a woman can alleviate some of the guilt or remorse she feels and be comforted that the Buddha will take care of the unborn babies in the afterlife.

Tiny statues surround Jizo, each representing an aborted foetus.

A woman tends the grave of a lost child. Many women feel the need to mourn after an abortion.

What is Post-traumatic Abortion Syndrome?

Many pro-life groups believe that a large percentage of women who have undergone an abortion experience serious depression, and massive feelings of guilt. This has been called Post-traumatic Abortion Syndrome, Post Abortion Syndrome and PAS. Every woman reacts in a different way. They each have different responses in different time frames. Some women repress or are unaware of any after effects for many years. Studies in the US report negative reactions to include feelings of guilt, shame, anxiety, helplessness, grief and remorse.

Can abortion bring about positive feelings?

Abortion can produce positive reactions too. Some women feel more in control of their lives following an abortion. They may feel stronger, more determined and more self-assertive. An abortion sometimes leaves women feeling more certain that she wants a child, but at the right time. She may also make a decision to practise safer sex and be much more aware of her bodily changes and her emotional and physical needs. In 1995, a Canadian survey was done of women who had recently chosen to terminate their first pregnancy at an early stage. It found that almost 80 per cent 'felt relief and satisfaction' soon after they had had the abortion.

Why Would A Woman Want An Abortion?

There are many reasons why women choose to have an abortion. Faced with an unwanted pregnancy, a woman may feel she is too young or too old to have a baby. Other women simply do not want children, or do not want to increase their family size. Some women have an abortion because of medical risks to themselves or because of serious foetal abnormality.

A teenager who finds out that she is pregnant may want to terminate a pregnancy because she feels that she is too young to have a baby.

RECENT DATA SHOWS that in the USA 52 per cent of pregnancies are intended (at the time of conception) and 48 per cent are unintended. There are approximately three million unintended pregnancies each year in the USA. Some 2.1 per cent of all women of child-bearing age (15–44) had an abortion in the year 2000. Most women, over 90 per cent, decide to have an abortion because of economic or personal reasons. About six per cent of all abortions are sought because of medical complications involving the woman or the foetus, and about one per cent of all abortions are sought because of an abusive sexual act.

What are the non-medical reasons for abortion?

Worldwide, 21 per cent of women are able to obtain legal abortions for social or economic reasons. Some countries, such as Afghanistan, Indonesia and Iran, prohibit abortion except for cases where the mother's life is endangered by the pregnancy. In countries such as the UK, USA and Scandinavian nations where

A woman may choose to terminate a pregnancy because she has a successful career, or feels that she is simply not ready to bring up a child.

abortion is obtainable to any woman who wants it, around 90 per cent of abortions take place for social reasons, such as financial wellbeing. Studies show that the most common reason for seeking an abortion is a fear that the woman cannot afford to look after a baby. Some 21 per cent of American women feel that they lack the financial resources to have a baby.

Many women who decide to have an abortion do so because they are not ready for the responsibility of bringing up a child, or they do not wish to have a baby at all. About 16 per cent believe that their life would be changed too much. Having a baby would be too disruptive to an important 'life-plan', such as a university or college course, a successful career or plans to travel. A woman may already be committed to looking after a sick partner or elderly parents and, therefore, feel that it is impossible to commit to the demands of a new baby.

Interesting comparisons

In some Islamic countries, abortion rates are low because couples want to have large families and also sex outside marriage brings severe penalties for women. In the Netherlands, the abortion rate is low for completely different reasons. Dutch women prefer small families and premarital sex is very common, but because of widespread use of effective contraception, abortion is uncommon.

Rape and pregnancy

About one per cent of all abortions are sought because of an abusive sexual act. In the US, between 10 000–15 000 abortions are sought each year because the conception occurred after rape or incest and the woman does not want to bear a child who was conceived in violence.

Source: Alan Guttmacher Institute

What about the role of a partner?

Some 12 per cent of women who want an abortion feel that their relationships with their partners are in difficulty or that the present relationship would be jeopardised by having a baby. The father of the foetus may not even be around, and the woman may feel unable to cope with having a child on her own, or feel that it is wrong to have a baby whose father will not be there to play an active role in bringing it up.

A woman who is struggling to bring up a large family may not want to have another child.

The use of contraceptives, such as these, has been shown to reduce abortion rates in a country.

According to the laws in the majority of countries where abortion is legal, the father's consent to an abortion is not needed. Some men have felt frustrated that their feelings are not considered when making the decision. On the other hand, some women feel that the pregnancy and the abortion only affect their body and that they alone should make such a decision. In societies that allow abortion on demand, however, most women would want to discuss their pregnancy with the father of the foetus.

Are abortion and contraception linked?

Contraceptive use around the world varies greatly. In some sub-Saharan countries, less than ten per cent of women of reproductive age use contraception, while in many developed countries around 75 per cent of women use it. Recent studies have shown that, generally, abortion rates are highest in societies where there is a desire for smaller families, where effective birth control methods are not practised and where induced abortion is relied on for birth control.

DEBATE - Should the baby's father have a say?

• Yes. The foetus is as much his as it is the mother's.

• No. It is the woman's body and her life that would be disrupted, not the man's.

Family planning programmes in many developing countries have helped to increase access to contraceptive services. This has led to fewer unwanted pregnancies and a subequent reduction in abortion rates. However, in countries where abortion is illegal and birth control inadequate, there are still high abortion rates, with correspondingly high mortality rates. Worldwide, there are 55 000 unsafe abortions a day, 95 per cent of which are in developing countries, causing the deaths of at least 200 women each day. Out of all the women in Latin America, Asia and Africa who are suffering complications from unsafe abortions, fewer than one-third have ever used contraceptives.

This woman is campaigning for the rights of disabled people. Disability rights campaigners feel that it is wrong to abort a baby on the grounds of a physical or mental disability.

What are the medical reasons for having an abortion?

Sometimes, a pregnant woman finds herself in circumstances which limit or take away her freedom to choose. She might be very ill, perhaps through an accident, and an abortion may be necessary to save her life. Other conditions which might threaten the health of the woman include severe heart and kidney disease. Similarly, through ultrasound scans (see page 43) a pregnant woman may learn from the doctor that her foetus is so damaged it would not survive birth. In this situation, the woman is likely to choose an abortion, although she may be a member of a religion that forbids abortion under any circumstances. In other cases, a woman may be told that her foetus will be born with serious physical or mental impairment. She then has a very difficult decision to make – to abort or keep the baby.

What causes foetal damage?

The foetus might have been harmed by exposure to infections, such as rubella (German measles), high radiation levels and high levels of toxic chemicals, including those found in some medicines. These substances can cause the foetus serious damage. One legal drug that caused great controversy in the early days of the abortion debate was thalidomide. Thalidomide was prescribed as a sedative and to relieve morning sickness in pregnant women. However, it was found to cause severe malformations in infants. There were several high-profile cases of women who had taken thalidomide and then opted to abort the damaged foetus, including that of Sheri Finkbine, who had to travel from her home in the US to Sweden in 1962 in order to have an abortion. Other causes of foetal damage include genetic defects, such as Down's syndrome, and inherited diseases.

Why shouldn't people with handicaps be born?

The access to a legal abortion on the grounds of foetal abnormality, where the baby will be born with a disability of some kind, has raised serious concerns among many people, including pro-life supporters and disability rights campaigners. These people believe that a disabled child can go on to lead a full life.

In December 2003, Joanna Jepson, a Church of England curate, questioned a case of an abortion of a foetus with a cleft palate (when the cells of the lips, face and palate fail to fuse together). The abortion had been carried out after the 24th week of the pregnancy, a time when, according to the UK Abortion Act, abortions are only allowed if a severe disability has been found in the foetus. In Jepson's opinion, the cleft palate did not amount to a serious disability.

Sheri Finkbine chose to have an abortion after she found out that the sedatives she took during pregnancy contained thalidomide.

Is Right-To-Life Or Right-To-Choose More Important?

Not everyone who has an opinion about abortion will take either a definite pro-choice or pro-life view. However, their thoughts and feelings about abortion issues will undoubtedly be influenced by the arguments of these two opposing sides.

These pro-choice campaigners are holding a candle-lit vigil outside the US Supreme Court to mark the 30th anniversary of the Roe v Wade ruling.

THOSE WHO ADVOCATE the 'right to choose' say that they should not be labelled 'pro-abortion' and that their arguments concern women's rights over their own bodies. The pro-life supporters maintain that because human life begins at conception then all abortions involve the killing of innocent children. There are, however, developments that are complicating some of the issues.

What are the complicating issues?

The issue of foetal viability – the point at which a foetus can survive outside the mother's body – is a key one in opening up the debate to complex new questions.

In the last 15 years or so, advances in medical technology have enabled women to give birth to very premature babies. Today, babies born at 21–22 weeks can be routinely saved and viability is now set at 19 weeks. This situation has forced people to reconsider the ethical issues surrounding late-term abortion.

Kenya King

On 16 June 1985, in Florida, USA, Kenya King was born at 21 weeks into her mother's pregnancy. She was over four months premature and weighed only 510 g. Kenya was kept in intensive care and when she left the hospital with her mother she weighed 2.25 kg. Since her birth, more babies have been born before the 22–24 week mark. The record for the most premature baby to survive is held by James Gill, who was born 128 days prematurely in May 1987.

What do pro-choice supporters believe?

Pro-choice supporters believe that abortion is not wrong in itself and should be far more widely available throughout the world. Contrary to the pro-life view, they tend not to acknowledge the foetus as a person, although they consider that from the embryonic stage there is 'potential life'. They argue, therefore, that it is not the rights of the foetus that are paramount but those of the pregnant woman. She should have legal authority over what happens to her body. They currently campaign for legalising abortion in countries where there are high rates of dangerous illegal abortions. They also maintain that if contraception and birth-control education were more widely available, far fewer abortions would happen worldwide.

A photo of Kenya King with her mother.

Should a woman have the right to choose an abortion?

Human rights laws protect pregnant women, but they do not automatically give them the right to have an abortion. Some women feel that they should and that abortion should be available on demand and with fewer legal restrictions, such as the need to refer to a second doctor. Women supporting the legalisation of abortion call themselves the pro-choice movement.

What are pro-choice arguments?

Pro-choice supporters maintain that no one has a right to limit a woman's freedom of choice or her freedom of action. They do not see why women should tolerate intervention from government, religious organisations, friends, family or members of the medical establishment on the question of whether or when they should be allowed to have an abortion. The pro-choice line of argument is that women have the right to control their own bodies. Pro-choice supporters also feel that a pregnant woman should not have to justify her reason or reasons in order to 'win' an abortion.

In their support of legal abortion, pro-choice groups claim that the embryo or foetus does not have the same value as

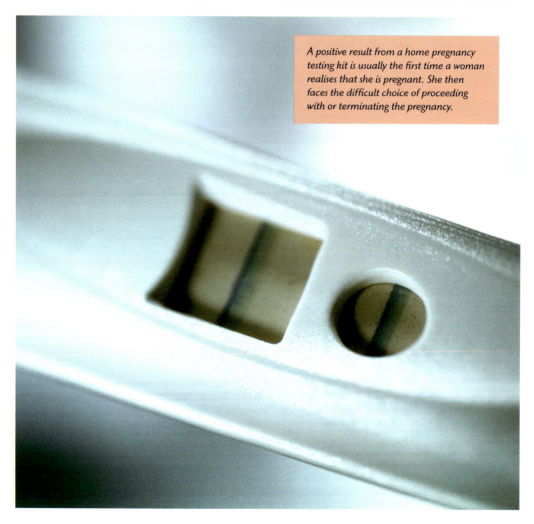

A positive result from a home pregnancy testing kit is usually the first time a woman realises that she is pregnant. She then faces the difficult choice of proceeding with or terminating the pregnancy.

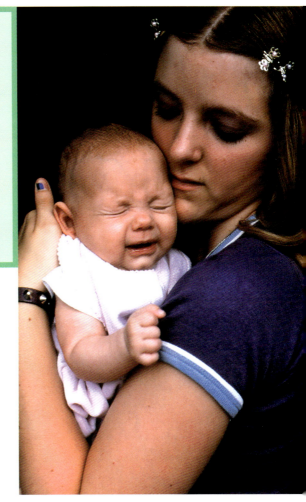

A young mother from the UK, where the declining rate of abortions has been blamed on a successful campaign by pro-life organisations.

a born person and that a woman is capable of making the right moral choice and that she can follow her own conscience. They also believe that a pregnant woman understands her own personal circumstances better than anyone else. They maintain that legal abortion is relatively safe and a woman will suffer more harm if she is forced to continue her pregnancy and have an unwanted child. Linked to this argument is their belief that children should be born to parents who want and love them. Unwanted babies, they claim, will lead to traumatised mothers, child abuse and more children being put into care. They also claim that making abortion illegal or socially unacceptable does not make it disappear. In states and countries where abortion is illegal, women who are desperate to end their pregnancy will seek unsafe illegal methods.

What other concerns do they have?

A major concern in the UK, especially, is the rise of teenage pregnancies with girls as young as 12 or 13 giving birth. Would better sex education and information about contraception and abortion help reduce currently high statistics? Some pro-choice supporters think so. In the UK, 63 in every 1000 girls under the age of 20 get pregnant every year. Only 37 per cent opt for abortion. About 50 per cent of all girls who get pregnant under 16 have abortions, and figures are rising. Recent surveys show that young girls are far more anti-abortion than older women. Pro-choice reformers believe this is due to information sent to schools by various pro-life groups.

Former US President Bill Clinton lifted the restrictions caused by the global gag rule.

Statistics

In Africa – where most countries have restrictive abortion laws – four million unsafe abortions occur each year and more than 40 per cent of the world's deaths due to unsafe abortions occur on the continent.

Are there pro-choice organisations in the developing world?

International organisations such as the United Nations, the Alliance of Family Planning and the International Planned Parenthood Federation are concerned about issues of women's reproductive health worldwide. They see several major areas of concern: the high mortality rates in childbirth in some countries; the lack of effective contraception which has accounted for the rapid spread of HIV/AIDS in some regions; the high rate of pregnancy among very young women; and the large number of illegal abortions and subsequent statistics of women who suffer the consequences of these.

Both contraception and abortion can be problematic subjects for communities in some cultures in the developing world, just as they are for many societies in developed nations. While there is certainly a need to control the spread of sexually transmitted diseases and to reduce the rate of illegal abortions, there is also a need to respect various cultural taboos, religious teachings and sexual practices in countries that are most vulnerable to HIV and AIDS and have high rates of illegal abortion. It is also vital to ensure that 'family planning' programmes are not part of a more sinister agenda which seeks to control populations by subjecting women to coercive birth control methods, including enforced abortion. Respecting women's reproductive rights is an important principle in the pro-choice campaign.

Part of the pro-choice international agenda is devoted to promoting access to safe legal abortion and to increasing the availability of effective contraception and sex education, which could lower the abortion rates. Certainly, in the past ten years, modern family planning methods have reduced abortion rates in some countries by 60 per cent. These countries include Russia, Hungary, Chile, Mexico, South Korea, Kazakhstan and Ukraine. The World Health Organisation, however, reports that 90 per cent of all unsafe abortions still happen in the developing world – South and Southeast Asia, sub-Saharan Africa, Latin America and the Caribbean.

What was the 'gag rule'?

The 'global gag rule' was a US government policy enacted in 1984 during the Reagan administration. It was also named the 'Mexico City' policy,

after a population conference held there. The 'rule' prohibited foreign non-governmental organisations that received US funds from speaking out for or against abortion laws or from providing legal abortion services, even if they used only their own funds or were engaged in democratic policy debate in their own countries. The gag rule was repealed by President Clinton during his first few days in office in January 1993, when he signed a document that lifted the restrictions.

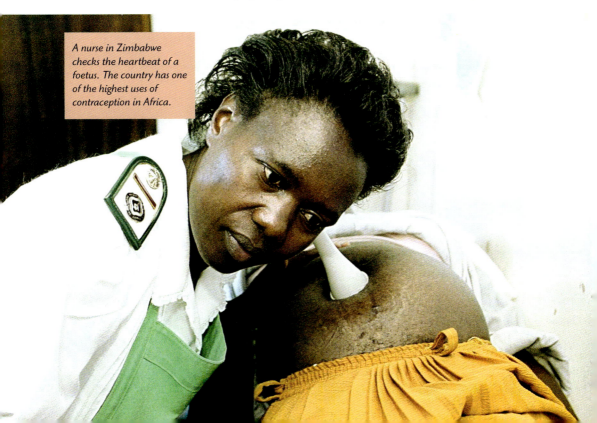

A nurse in Zimbabwe checks the heartbeat of a foetus. The country has one of the highest uses of contraception in Africa.

Eleanor Roosevelt holds up a copy of the United Nations Declaration of Human Rights.

What about the foetus' right to life?

Of all the major issues facing the world today, human rights is one of the most important. They were first listed in an international charter drawn up by the United Nations (UN) in 1948 and they guarantee basic rights for all men, women and children. There are now several charters and covenants in existence which protect human rights globally. One of the fundamental principles written in all of these charters is an article which states that every individual has the right to life.

It says that 'everyone has the right to life, liberty and security of person'.

Pro-life groups claim that abortion contravenes this fundamental right to life that is due every human being, including a foetus. They cite the World Medical Association's 1948 Declaration of Geneva, which contains a reformulation of the ancient Hippocratic oath. It states: 'I will maintain the utmost respect for human life, from the time of conception.'

Is there a strictly religious view on the right to life?

Many religions of different cultures support the basic tenet that an unborn foetus has a right to life. These diverse views vary in their degrees of tolerance towards abortion. Certain orthodox Jewish groups, for instance, are strictly pro-life. There are also various denominational groups in the Christian religion that are actively pro-life, including, for example, the Mormons. There are approximately 1000 conservative faith groups in North America that take a pro-life stand against abortion access. The Catholic Church says that human life begins at conception. In 1980, a document was issued by the seven Catholic Archbishops of Great Britain. It was called 'Abortion and the Right to Live' and it opposes all practices that degrade human rights and dignity. Abortion is seen as such a practice.

What else do the pro-life groups say?

They also claim that abortion causes psychological trauma to the mother and believe that abortion is rarely necessary to save the life of the woman. One pro-life report states that 'rape, incest, health of the baby and threat to the life or health of the mother combined, account for just seven per cent of all abortions in the US'. Organisations such as LIFE also fear that abortion on demand encourages far more casual sex among teenagers. As no contraceptive is 100 per cent effective, and many, they say, are abortifacients (a drug or agent that causes abortion), young people will use abortion as a simple solution to pregnancy.

A session of the United Nations, the organisation of countries formed after World War II which formulated the Declaration of Human Rights.

Norma McCorvey was the unidentified Jane Roe in the Roe v Wade case. Today, she is a pro-life supporter and campaigns vigorously. In June 2003, she filed to overturn the original Roe v Wade ruling.

Do pro-life groups accept abortion in exceptional circumstances?

Very few pro-life groups would outlaw abortion under all conditions, and almost all would permit abortion if continued pregnancy would cause the mother's death. Many would also allow an abortion if a pregnancy resulted from rape or incest. However, organisations such as LIFE, while condemning the act of rape, suggest that abortion can produce the same kind of feelings that a woman can feel after having been raped. They also see abortion as physically invasive and as potentially damaging as rape. They believe that a new life conceived through rape should not be extinguished through abortion, a further violent act.

But won't the mother hate the child when it is born?

LIFE believes that if the raped woman receives support and admiration from people around her she will be encouraged to continue her pregnancy and may feel emotionally stronger by doing so. The child conceived in rape is as valuable a person as any other child and will be loved regardless of the violent circumstances of its conception.

Do pro-life supporters see alternatives to abortion?

Yes. If a mother cannot cope physically, mentally, emotionally or economically, then there are many childless couples who would willingly adopt the unwanted baby. This includes babies born with disabilities. Pro-life groups also protest against abortion on grounds of foetal abnormality since they believe this encourages discrimination against disabled people. The Society for the Protection of Unborn Children (SPUC) maintains that abortion does not solve the social problems that lead women to seek abortion. Instead, it 'undermines the will of society... to find humane solutions which do not involve killing a baby.' One recent example in Scotland saw pro-life supporters offer money to women in order to stop them from having abortions.

3-D ultrasound

In 2003, images were published for the first time that seemed to suggest the foetus can smile, blink and cry at 26 weeks. The pictures have sparked off a debate as to whether the apparent 'grin' is reflecting an emotional response or whether it is a simple physical reaction. Some obstetricians believe the state-of-the-art scanning equipment that produces these 3-D ultrasound images is a major advance. It can help prepare parents for a baby's genetic defects and even show them that a physical 'deformity' in the foetus is actually much less serious than they thought.

DEBATE – Is the foetus' right to life the most important factor?

- Yes. The foetus has a basic right to life. Its destiny should not be decided by somebody else.

- No. A woman must have the right to choose what happens to her own body without interference from other people.

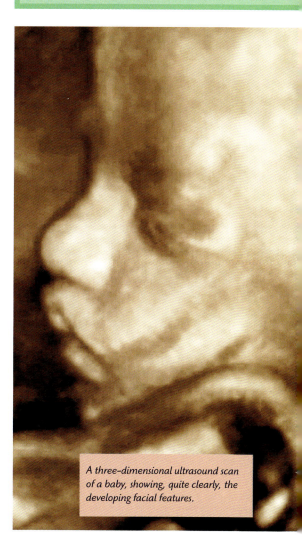

A three-dimensional ultrasound scan of a baby, showing, quite clearly, the developing facial features.

Where Is Abortion Legal?

There are varying degrees to which countries permit access to abortion. These conditions are covered, generally, by five categories, ranging from countries with the most restrictive laws to those with the most liberal legislation. In this chapter we will look at abortion's legal status on a global level and also consider what factors can affect the rates of abortion.

OF 193 COUNTRIES studied by the United Nations, four enforce bans in all circumstances, even if the life of the mother is threatened. Some 189 allow abortion to save the life of the mother and 122 countries permit abortion to protect the physical health of the mother. Some 120 allow an abortion to protect her mental health, 83 in the case of rape or incest, 76 allow abortion to eliminate a defective foetus and 52 allow it for economic or social reasons.

Where are the laws for abortion most restrictive?

According to the Center for Reproductive Rights, 72 nations (26.1 per cent of the world's population) have laws that permit abortion only to save a woman's life, or they ban the procedure entirely. In the United Nations' study, the four nations which ban abortion in all circumstances are Chile, El Salvador, Malta and the Vatican City (Rome). Other countries, including Nepal and Sao Tome and Principe, have bans that can be overridden by certain conditions.

Abortion is illegal in Nigeria, but thousands of women resort to it every year. Abortion rates are lower in North Nigeria, where this woman is from. Here people are poorer and the culture more traditional.

A busy street in Dublin, Ireland, which will only allow abortions to save a woman's life.

Polish laws not so permissive

Poland is the only European country that permits abortion to occur only in cases of high risk to the life of the woman. In January 1997, an amended abortion law was introduced which allowed women in difficult living conditions to have abortions. However, these rights to have an abortion on socio-economic grounds were then cancelled in December 1997. The earlier amendments were declared 'illegal' since they violated the constitution's protection of the right to life of the 'conceived child'.

Do European countries have the most permissive laws?

No, not necessarily. Abortion laws are still very restrictive in Cyprus, Israel, Poland, Portugal and Spain, where it is permitted only in cases of rape or foetal impairment, or to protect a woman's physical or mental health. The European nations that impose significant limitations on abortion are predominantly Catholic. The Republic of Ireland's abortion policy is very restrictive and only allows abortion to save a woman's life. Irish women now have the right to travel to the UK for an abortion under some circumstances.

Where can women obtain abortion on demand?

These countries include the USA, Canada, Singapore, South Korea, Tunisia and Turkey, as well as ten former Eastern bloc states and six Western European states. The communist countries Cuba, Mongolia, Vietnam, North Korea and the People's Republic of China are also included in this group. Even in the most permissive states, however, the laws still impose gestational limits and additional requirements such as parental consent for young girls. Saudi Arabia, Nepal and China also have specific laws banning abortion on the basis of sex selection.

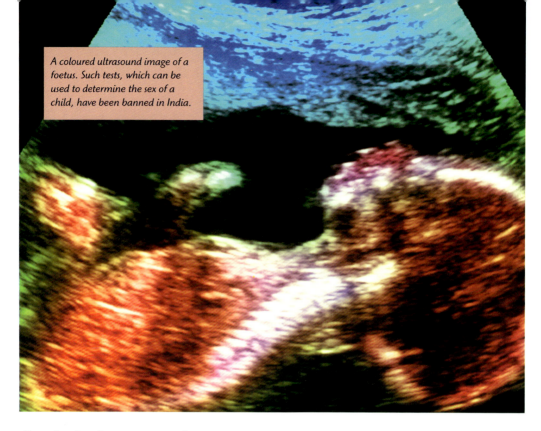

A coloured ultrasound image of a foetus. Such tests, which can be used to determine the sex of a child, have been banned in India.

How do abortion rates vary from country to country?

Recent studies indicate that abortion rates are no lower in countries where abortion is restricted by law, and, consequently, where many unsafe illegal abortions are performed than in regions where abortion is legally available. Surveys also show that both developed and developing countries can have low abortion rates.

There are a number of factors that account for the significant variations among regions. Worldwide, an estimated 58 per cent of unintended pregnancies end in abortion. This proportion is higher in the developed world (73 per cent) than in the developing world (54 per cent). The overall figures range from a high of 91 per cent in Eastern Europe to a low of 41 per cent in parts of Africa. Overall, the lowest abortion rates are found in Western Europe. A survey in 1999 showed that among countries where abortion is legal, the highest abortion rate, some 83 in 1000 women, was found in Vietnam, while the lowest of seven per 1000 women, was found in Belgium and the Netherlands.

Why are there such variations?

Studies in 2000 indicated that abortion rates are generally higher in societies where small families are desired and in societies where there is low use of effective contraception combined with low fertility standards. Relatively low abortion rates are found in regions where there are high levels of effective contraceptive use or where there is high desired fertility. Research also indicates that US women who use an effective method of contraception are 85 per cent less likely to have an abortion than sexually active women who are using no contraceptives at all.

How can governments control abortion rates?

It is clear that, while prohibitive laws do not ensure low abortion rates, neither does a more permissive legislation. International family planning organisations and pro-choice groups are adamant that an increase in contraceptive availability and use significantly reduces abortion rates. Studies in 1997 show that the abortion rates in Bogota, Colombia, and Mexico City fell significantly as contraceptive use doubled over a ten-year period.

In parts of India, a preference for sons has led to an increase in the practice of killing baby girls, although this has been illegal for more than 100 years. The development of sex determination has encouraged the practice of aborting female foetuses. India outlawed prenatal sex-determination tests in 1996 as ultrasound technology began to spread with a correlating decline in the number of girls born. In extreme circumstances, some countries, notably China, have imposed compulsory abortions in order to limit population growth (see below).

A mother and child in China. The country has banned parents from having more than one child in order to control the country's population growth. This law is enforced with compulsory abortion and sterilisation.

Romania

In Romania, in 1989, an estimated 86 per cent of maternal deaths was due to unsafe abortions. In the first year after legalisation of abortion, maternal deaths fell 40 per cent. Then, when the use of contraceptives more than doubled between 1993 and 1999, the abortion rate decreased by 35 per cent and abortion-related maternal mortality dropped by more than 80 per cent.

Source: United Nations Population Fund (UNFPA)

Pro–life demonstrators have sometimes been accused of blocking clinic entrances, threatening doctors, patients and staff, and destroying equipment.

What are the current pro-life activities and campaigns?

The Society for the Protection of Unborn Children (SPUC) has lobbied Parliament in the UK in protest at moves by pro-choice groups to liberalise the current UK abortion laws. The SPUC believes that the pro-choice groups aim to 'de-medicalise' abortion practice and therefore endanger the lives of pregnant women.

They are particularly against the idea of non-hospital nurses performing non-surgical abortions using the drug RU-486/prostaglandin.

The Pro-Life Action League based in Illinois, USA, has ongoing protests outside clinics where they display graphic abortion signs. The League also co-sponsors the annual 'SpeakOut Illinois Conference', a coalition of pro-life groups.

Pro-Life Activities is another US-based organisation founded by US Catholic bishops. They develop education material on abortion, cloning, embryo research, contraception and stem cell research, all of which they oppose. They conduct campaigns in Catholic churches and public squares.

What are the current campaigns among pro-choice organisations?

The Feminists Majority Foundation (FMF) is a US-based organisation which runs campaigns nationally and worldwide on issues of human rights, including abortion. They have conducted a ten-year public education campaign to make mifepristone available to women for early abortions. They also petition for 'Emergency Contraception Over the Counter'.

The Pacific Institute for Women's Health implements programmes that support organisations and media campaigns in developing countries where there are high rates of unsafe abortions and HIV / AIDS. They run clinics and centres in Africa, Asia, the Middle East, Latin America and the US.

Marie Stopes International (MSI) operates on a national level in the UK and globally. Their global campaigns have included 'Overturning the Global Gag Rule', which was reintroduced by President George W Bush in January 2001 (see page 51).

Some pro-choice groups, such as Marie Stopes, are also members of the Voice for Choice Campaign. This lobbies for abortion laws to be amended so that women can obtain abortion on demand in the early stages of pregnancy. It also calls for only one doctor's approval for abortions from 15–24 weeks and for doctors to declare any conscientious objection to performing abortions.

Floating abortion clinic

Women on Waves is a Dutch-founded organisation that operates a mobile clinic on a ship. It sails to countries where abortion is illegal, at the invitation of local women's organisations. Their policy is to provide safe, legal and professional abortion procedures. Some people are concerned that this creates controversy by ignoring the rules of other countries.

On 22 January 2003, the 30th anniversary of the Roe v Wade decision, pro–choice activists gathered to demand that abortion be kept safe and legal.

What Is The Future For Abortion?

To an outsider, very little appears to have changed to the attitudes of supporters of both sides of the abortion debate. If anything, it could be argued that both sides have become more entrenched in their views. Nevertheless, both sides can claim successes in influencing issues in several countries.

Hillary Clinton is a pro–choice advocate, supporting the right to safe, legal abortion. She believes in improving family planning and access to healthcare worldwide.

DEBATE – Should the media take a more prominent role in the debate?

- Yes. People would be able to discuss the issues more rationally.
- No. The media are incapable of being objective and tend to politicise debates like this.

Are some countries becoming more tolerant in their attitude?

Yes, Switzerland has introduced more liberal legislation. In October 2002, the Swiss people voted to decriminalise abortion in two referendums called to decide whether to liberalise the country's 66-year-old law, or to toughen it further. The final results from one referendum show that 72 per cent of voters backed a parliamentary measure to allow abortions within the first 12 weeks of

Dr Barnett Slepian was murdered by a pro-life supporter for performing abortions.

Nuremburg File

In the 1990s, an American organisation ran the 'Nuremburg File' website, which listed the names of doctors willing to carry out abortions. When some of these doctors were murdered by anti-abortion protesters, their names appeared crossed out on the website list. Critics accused the website organisers of threatening the other doctors named on the list, and encouraging anti-abortion supporters to murder them.

pregnancy. In the other, 82 per cent of voters rejected a proposal by anti-abortion groups to toughen Switzerland's already strict abortion laws.

Are some countries becoming less liberal?

On his first day in office in 2001, which coincided with the 28th anniversary of the Roe v Wade decision legalising abortion nationwide, President George W Bush reinstated the 'global gag rule'. This requires that indigenous non-governmental organisations overseas promise not to use their own funds to pursue efforts to make abortion legal in their country, in return for US family planning assistance. His spokesman explained that the president believes this policy will 'make abortion more rare'.

To what extremes are people prepared to go?

In recent years, there have been cases of anti-abortionists going to extreme measures to stop abortions from taking place. There have been several cases of abortion supporters and doctors being murdered. In 1994, Florida-based doctor Paul Hill was shot dead by John Britton, who believed he was 'killing to save the unborn'. Britton was sentenced to death and executed by lethal injection in September 2003. In October 1998, Dr Barnett Slepian was shot in the back while standing in his kitchen in Buffalo, USA. Slepian's name was crossed out on 'The Nuremburg File' website later that same day.

REFERENCE

Abortion policy (1999)	Number of countries	Number of territories	Total population (2003)	Percentage of world population
Abortion on demand, sometimes mandatory	3	0	1 391 100 000	22.1
Abortion on demand	50	15	1 169 300 000	18.6
Abortion for economic or social reasons and in hard cases*	11	0	1 254 800 000	19.9
Abortion in some or all hard cases*	61	6	1 345 500 000	21.3
Abortion only to save mother's life or banned altogether	67	0	1 138 400 000	18.1
Unknown	1	26	3 500 000	0.1
Unpopulated territories	0	22	0	0.0
World totals	193	69	6 162 092 000	100.0

* hard cases include to protect the mother's physical or mental health, in cases of rape or incest, or to eliminate unhealthy babies.

Sources: *World Abortion Policies* Population Division of the United Nations Secretariat 1999

GROUNDS ON WHICH ABORTION IS PERMITTED IN MORE DEVELOPED AND LESS DEVELOPED REGIONS

Region	To save the woman's life	To preserve physical health	To preserve mental health	Rape or incest	Foetal impair-ment	Economic or social reasons	On request*
TOTAL							
COUNTRIES	193	193	193	193	193	193	193
Permitted	189	122	120	83	76	63	52
Not permitted	4	71	73	110	117	130	141
MORE							
DEVELOPED							
REGIONS	48	48	48	48	48	48	48
Permitted	46	42	41	39	39	36	31
Not permitted	2	6	7	9	9	12	17
LESS							
DEVELOPED							
REGIONS	145	145	145	145	145	145	145
Permitted	143	80	79	44	37	27	21
Not permitted	2	65	66	101	108	118	124

* For purposes of this table, if an abortion is authorised on request, it is presumed that an abortion can be performed during the period when it is authorised on request on any of the grounds listed, even if the law does not specifically mention such a ground.

Source: *Abortion Policies: An International Overview* (United Nations publication)

THE EFFECT OF EMERGENCY CONTRACEPTION ON THE NUMBER OF ABORTIONS

• The Alan Guttmacher Institute estimates that the total number of abortions was 1.4 million in 1994 and 1.3 million in 2000 – a reduction of 110,000 abortions or 11 per cent.

• In their 1994 survey of women who had an abortion, the institute found 1400 who had become pregnant in spite of using emergency contraception (EC). Thus, they estimated that three times as many women (4200 in total) had successfully used EC and had avoided becoming pregnant and having an abortion.

• In 1998, a more convenient form of EC, *Preven*, became available. In 1999, a second specially packaged EC came on the market. EC usage became much more common.

• In their year 2000 survey, the institute found 17 000 women who had become pregnant in spite of having using EC. They computed that 51 000 women had prevented pregnancy and a subsequent abortion in the year 2000 by using EC.

• The study concluded that the growth in emergency contraceptive usage was responsible for up to 43 per cent of the decline in the number of abortions from 1994 to 2000.

• It is generally acknowledged that this medication is about 75 per cent effective in preventing pregnancy.

Source: Alan Guttmacher Institute

ABORTION STATISITCS AROUND THE WORLD

Abortion statistics – world
- In 54 countries (61 per cent of the world's population) abortions are legal.
- In 97 countries (39 per cent of the world's population) abortions are illegal.
- There are approximately 46 million abortions conducted each year.
- There are approximately 126 000 abortions conducted each day.

Abortion statistics – US
- According to the Alan Guttmacher Institute, 1 370 000 abortions occur annually in the US.
- 88 per cent of abortions occur during the first six to 12 weeks of pregnancy.
- 47 per cent of abortions are performed on women who have already had one or more abortions.
- 43 per cent of women will have had at least one abortion by the time they are 45 years old.

Abortion statistics – demographics
- Age – The majority of women getting an abortion are young. 55 per cent are less than 26 years old and 21 per cent are teenagers. The abortion rate is highest for those women aged 18 to 19 (56 per 1000 in 1992).
- Marriage – 51 per cent of women who are unmarried when they become pregnant will receive an abortion. Unmarried women are six times more likely than married women to have an abortion.
- Race – 63 per cent of abortion patients are white. However, the abortion rate for non-white women is more than double that of white women.

Abortion statistics – decision to have an abortion (US)
- 25.5 per cent of women deciding to have an abortion want to postpone childbearing.
- 21.3 per cent of women cannot afford a baby.
- 14.1 per cent of women have a relationship issue or their partner does not want a child.
- 12.2 per cent of women are too young (their parents or others object to the pregnancy).
- 10.8 per cent of women feel a child will disrupt their education or career.
- 7.9 per cent of women want no (more) children.
- 3.3 per cent of women have an abortion due to a risk to foetal health.
- 2.8 per ccent of women have an abortion due to a risk to maternal health.

Abortion statistics – pro-life v pro-choice
- According to a *USA Today*, CNN Gallup Poll in May 1999, 16 per cent of Americans believe abortion should be legal for any reason at any time during pregnancy and 55 per cent of Americans believe abortion should be legal only to save the life of the mother or in cases of rape or incest.
- According to a Gallup Poll in January 2001, people who considered themselves to be pro-life rose from 33 per cent to 43 per cent in the previous five years, and people who considered themselves to be pro-choice declined from 56 per cent to 48 per cent.

Sources: Alan Guttmacher Institute and Pregnant Pause

GLOSSARY

abortifacient Medication which terminates a pregnancy and causes an abortion to happen.

abortion The word used to describe the end of a pregnancy.

accidental abortion A termination of pregnancy before viability that occurs naturally, without medical intervention. This is a medical term for a miscarriage.

anti-abortion This is a term with no fixed meaning. Sometimes it is used as a derogatory term for pro-life supporters.

baby A very young child aged from birth to perhaps one year. The term is sometimes used to refer to a zygote, blastocyst, morula, embryo or foetus.

blastocyst A stage of pre-natal mammalian development which (in humans) extends from the morula stage to the embryo stage (from about one week after fertilisation).

child Normally, this means a person aged from birth to puberty. Sometimes it is used to refer to an unborn foetus as well, particularly by pro-life advocates.

clinic A medical building where patients are treated or prescribed drugs.

colony An overseas territory that is governed by another country.

conception Another word for fertilisation, the fusing of sperm and egg.

embryo A stage of pre-natal development which, in humans, extends from two to eight weeks after fertilisation. From nine weeks, it is referred to as a foetus.

eugenics The study of 'improving' the quality of the human race through selective breeding, abortion, sterilisation and euthanasia.

fertilisation The process that starts when a sperm contacts an ovum. It ends with the fusion of genetic material from both the sperm and ovum. The result is a zygote.

foetus A stage of pre-natal development which, in humans, extends from nine weeks after fertilisation until birth.

Hippocratic oath An oath taken by a doctor upon graduating to observe a code of medical ethics. It is based on the teachings of the Ancient Greek doctor Hippocrates.

implantation Attachment of the embryo to the wall of the uterus. This is generally regarded as the start of pregnancy by medical professionals and the pro-choice movement.

infant A child; variously defined as aged from birth to one year, or to seven years, and even, in some legal applications, as old as 21 years.

Medicaid A health assistance programme in the USA which is used to pay for hospitals and the medical costs of poor people. It is funded by taxes.

microscope An instrument that uses lenses to magnify an object.

miscarriage Interruption of pregnancy before the seventh month. Usually used to refer to an expulsion of the foetus that starts without the intervention of a doctor. Approximately one-quarter of all pregnancies end in a miscarriage.

morula A very early stage of pre-natal development in mammals. This stage starts when the zygote has developed into a mass of 16 cells. This is typically four days after fertilisation, and about ten days before it becomes implanted in the wall of the womb.

ovum The mature sex cell generated by females in an ovary. They are often (although not necessarily) released from alternate ovaries about once per month.

period Also called menstruation, this is the time when an unfertilised egg and the built-up lining of the womb are expelled by the woman's body. It occurs approximately every 28 days.

placenta The organ which links the foetus to the blood supply of the mother. Through the placenta pass the oxygen and nutrients necessary for the foetus to develop.

pregnancy The medical and pro-choice communities see this as the stages of pre-natal development that extend from the time that the embryo attaches to the wall of the uterus until birth. Pregnancy thus starts about two weeks after conception. Pro-life groups see pregnancy as extending from fertilisation to birth.

pre-natal A term to describe a stage before a baby's birth.

pro-choice A belief that women should be given free access to abortions if they wish to terminate a pregnancy. Some pro-choice people believe that a woman should have free access to abortions up until foetal viability; others say that a woman should be able to choose to have an abortion later in pregnancy.

pro-life A belief that life begins at the instant of conception (or perhaps shortly after, when a unique mix of genetic material is produced by the fusion of the two sex cells) and that it should be protected under law from that point.

sperm The mature sex cell generated by males. Almost all of their length is formed by a tail. Tens of thousands are generated every minute by most males, starting at puberty, but only one is needed to fertilise an egg.

sub-Saharan Africa The area of Africa whose countries lie south of the Sahara desert.

therapeutic abortion A termination of pregnancy via the intervention of a doctor through surgery or the use of the drug RU-486 or some other medication.

trimester A period lasting nominally three months. A human pregnancy is often divided into three trimesters, from fertilisation to birth.

umbilical cord A cord which attaches the foetus to the placenta and through which pass oxygen and nutrients from the mother to help the foetus develop.

uterus Another word for the womb, this is the women's organ inside which a fertilised egg implants and develops into a foetus.

vagina The female sexual organs.

viability The ability for the developing foetus to live outside its mother's womb. This typically occurs sometime after the 21st week after conception.

zygote A recently fertilised ovum.

FURTHER INFORMATION

BOOKS

What Do I Do Now? Talking About Teen Pregnancy, Susan Kuklin, Universal Publishers 2001

Abortion (Opposing Viewpoints) Mary E Williams, Greenhaven Press 2001

Kids Still Having Kids: Talking about Teen Pregnancy, Janet Bode, et al, Franklin Watts 1999

Pregnancy (Teen Decisions), William Dudley (ed), Lucent Books 2001

Teens and Pregnancy (Hot Issues), Ann Byers, Enslow Publishers 2000

Tough Choices, Alison Hadley, The Women's Press 1999

Teen Fathers Today, Ted Gottfried, Twenty-First Century Books (CT) 2001

Teenage Pregnancy (Opposing Viewpoints), Auriana Ojeda (ed), Greenhaven Press 2002

Surviving Teen Pregnancy: Your Choices, Dreams and Decisions, Shirley Arthur, Perry Bergman (illustrator), Morning Glory 1996

Overcoming Feelings of Hatred (Focus on Family Matters), Michele Alpern, Chelsea House Publications 2002

Teen Pregnancy (Focus on Family Matters), Michele Alpern, Chelsea House Publications 2002

ORGANISATIONS

Pro-choice organisations:
National Abortion Campaign (NAC)
The Print House
18 Ashwin Street
London E8 3DL
Tel: 020 7923 4976
http://www.gn.apc.org/nac

Feminist Women's Health Center
14220 Interurban Avenue South #140
Seattle, WA 98168
USA
E-mail: info@fwhc.org

NARAL: Pro-Choice California
32 Monterey Boulevard
San Francisco, CA 94131
USA
Tel: +1 415 334 1502
Fax: +1 415 334 6510
E-mail: info@prochoicecalifornia.org

Pro-life organisations:
LIFE
LIFE House, Newbold Terrace,
Leamington Spa
Warwickshire CV32 4EA
Tel: 01926 421 587
http://www.lifeuk.org

National Women's Coalition for Life
NWCL National Headquarters:
PO Box 1553 Oak Park,
IL 60304
USA
Tel: +1 708 848 5351

Feminists for Life
733 15th Street, NW
Suite 1100
Washington DC 20005
USA
Tel: +1 202 737 3352

WEBSITES

Pro-choice websites:

http://www.fwhc.org
The Feminist Women's Health Center maintains an extensive website with information about abortion procedures, personal stories and poetry.

http://www.matisse.net/politics/caral/abortion.html
The California Abortion and Reproductive Rights Action League (CARAL) page lists 13 pro-choice sites, 18 of what they call 'anti-choice' sites, as well as a list of important historical documents and essays.

http://www.plannedparenthood.org
Planned Parenthood Online has information on abortion – how to decide whether abortion is right for you, descriptions of the procedure and its risks and supporting information for friends, parents or partners of a woman seeking abortion.

http://www.infidels.org/org/ffrf/nontracts/abortion.html
The Secular Web has a list of religious denominations in the US that support women's access to abortion.

Pro-life websites:

http://www.GodlessProlifers.org
The Atheist and Agnostic Pro-Life League is one of the few pro-life groups that is not based on conservative Christianity.

http://www.feministsforlife.org
Feminists for Life of America bill themselves as pro-woman and pro-life. The group opposes 'all forms of violence – including abortion, infanticide, child abuse, domestic violence, assisted suicide, euthanasia and capital punishment.'

http://www.l4l.org
Libertarians for Life argues on the pro-life side from a Libertarian position.

http://www.nrlc.org
National Right to Life deals with many pro-life causes, but concentrates on abortion matters.

http://www.sehlat.com/lifelink/ffl/plgroups.html
National Women's Coalition for Life is 'an umbrella organisation for national women's groups that oppose abortion.'

INDEX

Marie Stopes
  International 49
McCorvey, Norma 42
Medicaid 17, 56
medical abortions 22, 23
methotrexate 22
Mexico 39
Mexico City 46
microscopes 13, 56
Middle East, the 12, 49
Mifeprex 22
mifepristone 22
miscarriages 10, 22, 25,
  56
misoprostol 22, 25
Mongolia 45
morulas 19, 56, 57
mothers 10, 20, 21, 34, 35,
  43, 44, 57
Muslims 13

Nepal 44, 45
Netherlands, the 9, 29, 46
New Jersey 15
New York 16
Nigeria 25, 44
North Korea 45
Nuremburg File, The 51
nurses 25, 36

ova *see* eggs
ovaries 18, 23, 57

Pacific Institute for
  Women's Health 49
periods 18, 19, 57
Philippines 25
Pius IX, Pope 14
placentas 19, 57
Poland 45
police 8, 9
Portugal 45
post-abortion counsellor
  26
Post-traumatic Abortion
  Syndrome 27

pregnancies 9, 10, 11, 12,
  13, 16, 17, 18, 19, 22, 24,
  25, 26, 28, 30, 31, 33, 35,
  37, 38, 41, 42, 46, 54, 55,
  56, 57
pro-choice groups 16, 34,
  35, 36, 37, 38, 39, 47, 49,
  50, 56, 57
Pro-Life Action League
  48
Pro-Life Activities 48
pro-life groups 10, 23, 25,
  33, 34, 35, 40, 41, 42, 43,
  48, 51, 56, 57
psychological effects 22,
  26, 41
puberty 18, 56, 57

quickening 20

rape 8, 9, 30, 41, 42, 44, 53
referendums 50
Roe v Wade 17, 34, 42, 49,
  51
Roman Catholicism 9, 14,
  20, 41, 48, 45
Romania 47
Rome 13
Roosevelt, Eleanor 40
RU-486 22, 48, 57
rubella 33
Russia 39

Sao Tome and Principe
  44
Saudi Arabia 45
Singapore 45
Slepian, Dr Barnett 51
Society for the Protection
  of the Unborn Child
  (SPUC) 43, 48
souls 12, 13, 14, 21
South Africa 25
South America 15
South Korea 39, 45
Spain 25, 45

sperm 13, 18, 19, 20, 56,
  57
sterilisation 14, 47, 56
surgical abortions 22, 23
Sweden 33
Switzerland 50, 51

teenagers 28, 41
testes 18
thalidomide 33
Tunisia 45
Turkey 45

UK 8, 16, 17, 19, 24, 26,
  28, 37, 45, 48, 49
Ukraine 39
ultrasound 42, 43, 46, 47
umbilical cord 19, 57
United Nations (UN) 38,
  40, 41, 44
  Declaration of Human
  Rights 40, 41
USA 14, 15, 16, 17, 19, 22,
  24, 27, 28, 30, 33, 35, 38,
  39, 45, 46, 48, 49, 51, 55,
  56
US Congress 17
US Supreme Court 17, 34

vacuum aspiration 22
vaginas 22, 57
Vatican City 44
viability 20, 21, 34, 35, 57
Vietnam 45, 46

wombs 18, 19, 20, 21, 22,
  23, 24, 56, 57
Women on Waves 49
women's rights 15, 16
World Medical
  Association 40

Zacchia, Paolo 13
Zambia 9
Zimbabwe 24, 39
zygotes 19, 56, 57